D1168901

Graduating From Guilt

Six Steps to Overcome Guilt and Reclaim Your Life

By Holly Michelle Eckert

CNVC Certified Trainer

PuddleDancer
PRESS

P.O. Box 231129, Encinitas, CA 92023-1129
email@PuddleDancer.com • www.PuddleDancer.com

For additional information:
Center for Nonviolent Communication
5600 San Francisco Rd. NE, Suite A, Albuquerque, NM 87109
Ph: 505-244-4041 • Fax: 505-247-0414 • Email: cnvc@cnvc.org • Website: www.cnvc.org

Graduating From Guilt
Six Steps to Overcome Guilt and Reclaim Your Life

ISBN: 978-1-892005-23-6

Author: Holly Michelle Eckert

Editor: Kyra Freestar

Indexer: Phyllis Linn

Cover and Interior Design: Lightbourne, www.lightbourne.com

Cover photo: www.istock.com

Requests for permission should be addressed to:

PuddleDancer Press
Permissions Dept.
P.O. Box 231129
Encinitas, CA 92023-1129
Fax: 858-759-6967
email@PuddleDancer.com

Contents

Acknowledgments

This book is a result of the synergy of an entire community. In particular, I would like to thank:

Marshall Rosenberg, founder of Nonviolent Communication (NVC), for showing me the door to a new world,

Dana Gaskin Wenig, who first introduced me to NVC,

Seattle trainers Doug Dolstad, Liv Monroe, and Barbara Larson, for their support on my NVC journey from the beginning to the present,

My mother, for thirty-nine years of unwavering and wholehearted dedication to my educational and creative pursuits,

My father, who told me that I was smart enough to be successful at anything I set out to do,

My husband, who has supported my NVC journey financially, emotionally, and logistically, every step of the way,

My children, who inspired my passion to learn NVC and give me unintentional yet consistent feedback on how I'm doing in my learning process,

My extended family, for the countless hours of babysitting and enthusiastic cheerleading of my projects,

All my class participants over the years, whose feedback inspired me to continue developing my materials,

My editor, Kyra Freestar, for her impeccable standards and gentle introduction to the editing process,

The Center for Nonviolent Communication, for creating an infrastructure through which NVC is shared around the globe,

PuddleDancer Press, for sharing my enthusiasm for this book and distributing the NVC materials throughout the world, and

My writing coach, Waverly Fitzgerald, who showed me the path from concept to reality.

Endorsements for *Graduating From Guilt*

"With clear, engaging writing, this short but compelling book lives up to its title, offering six steps to 'graduate' from feelings of guilt and regret. The ideas are general enough to be useful in any situation, with interesting, specific examples and stories to help bring it all home. I highly recommend this profoundly important book and plan to use it often in my counseling practice."

—JAN HUNT, M.Sc., parenting counselor and author of
The Natural Child: Parenting From the Heart

"Many people think of Nonviolent Communication (NVC) as solely a communication tool when it is actually a vehicle for deep inner transformation. If your relationship with yourself isn't loving and connected, or if you are at war with yourself, then all of your relationships will suffer. Holly Eckert understands this, and her book is a wonderful and systematic teaching on how NVC can be used to transform inner consciousness. I will definitely be recommending this book to my therapy clients and students and know they will benefit from its wisdom and practical examples."

—MARK J. GOODMAN, MA, mindfulness-based psychotherapist,
faculty member at the Leadership Institute of Seattle (LIOS)
Graduate College of Saybrook University, training future
psychotherapist, business coaches and consultants

"Reading about guilt may not sound like a fascinating and hopeful subject, but Holly makes it so. In this straightforward and yet profound volume, you will be surprised with both the simplicity and profundity of her methodology. Highly recommended for those who want to learn to live more lightly and hopefully in all relationships."

—JUDITH HANSON LASATER, Ph.D., PT, yoga teacher since 1971
and coauthor (with Ike K. Lasater) of *What We Say Matters:
Practicing Nonviolent Communication*

"*Graduating From Guilt* offers a clear pathway for letting go of any old programming around guilt. If there is anything in your world where you are feeling stuck, I invite you to allow this process to contribute to your wholeness and well-being now."

—SANDY FOX, founder, Seattle Center For Peace

"*Graduating From Guilt* offers a simple six-step process for overcoming guilt gently, easily, and effectively. Eckert's approach is clear and direct, insightful and creative, warm as a summer breeze, and yet powerful enough to move mountains of painful emotion. If you're looking for a book to help free your heart, *Graduating From Guilt* is a great choice!"

—CAT SAUNDERS, Ph.D., author of *Dr. Cat's Helping Handbook: A Compassionate Guide for Being Human*

"*Graduating From Guilt* is a wise, unique, and beautifully written guidebook for those who want to release the quagmire their guilt leaves them in. Holly's Six Steps to Overcome Guilt are simple, practical, and yet profoundly life changing."

—MARY MACKENZIE, international peacemaker, author of *Peaceful Living*, and co-founder of the NVC Academy

"I find this book marvelously clear and accessible, and recommend it widely. I appreciate the diversity of situations represented, and imagine readers feeling immediately encouraged and confident in walking their own situation through the clearly delineated process. This is a great contribution, Holly, and I thank you for the care you have taken to offer your teaching and experience in a form that will benefit so many of us."

—LUCY LEU, co-founder, Freedom Project and Freedom Project Canada, and coauthor, *Nonviolent Communication Toolkit for Facilitators*

"What I love about this book is that it's so practical! NVC is a lot easier to understand than it is to do, but Holly offers a crystal clear, step-by-step process that really is easy to follow. The stories are rich and alive and open up a whole range of ideas of how and when to use her Graduating From Guilt process."

—MIRIAM DYAK, co-founder, The Voice Dialogue Institute

Introduction

Six Steps to Freedom

How can we free ourselves from the guilt that drains our creativity, joy, and aliveness? Is there a way to be accountable for our actions without beating ourselves up? Is it possible that guilt has a positive purpose in our lives? What might that be?

You likely find your response to your own guilt unpleasant. When feeling guilty, you might continually replay situations in your mind without any resolution. You might avoid the other people involved. You might pretend that nothing happened. You might attempt an apology, but still be left with lingering feelings that you've done something wrong. You might carry this guilt for days, months, years, even decades. All these options leave you stuck, judging yourself, living in the past, and disconnected from your authenticity, relationships, and presence.

Through living and teaching Nonviolent Communication (NVC) for the past nine years, I have accessed a completely different response to guilt. Guilt transformed through the six-step process explained here becomes an asset. Imagine that the next time you find yourself feeling guilty, you also feel eager to move through the six steps and into the gifts of greater authenticity and integrity!

During the last five years, I've guided hundreds of people through the process of Graduating From Guilt. In most cases, the guilt is 100 percent released in about twenty minutes. In a few deeper or longer-standing situations, participants reported feeling at least 80 percent less guilty—thus gaining much more lightness, freedom, and empowerment.

I find that laying out the whole process visually brings me clarity. In the Graduating From Guilt class, we create a large worksheet on a flip chart for reference. While the examples in this book are described in prose, I have also included a completed Graduating From Guilt worksheet at the end of each chapter. At the end of the book, on page 77, you will find a blank Graduating From Guilt worksheet for your own use.

I suggest that you read through the introduction to the six steps and at least two or three of the examples to get an overview of the process before working through your own situation. When you are ready to guide yourself through the steps, you might want a quiet space where you can really embrace the feelings that come up and experience the needs in your body. This will give you the maximum benefit of this full-body transformative process.

Step 1: Identify the Guilt

The first step in the Graduating From Guilt process is to define what you feel guilty about. It could be a specific action that you took (I yelled at my brother), an action that you failed to take (I didn't report my suspicions of domestic violence, and now my neighbor is in the hospital), or a general topic (I feel guilty about being a bad parent, an unappreciative child, or an irresponsible global citizen).

• • •

One day a woman, let's call her Jenny,[1] arrived at a Graduating From Guilt class and stated that she was feeling guilty about attending the guilt class. When we asked her to tell us more, she revealed that she had come straight to the class from work: She was feeling guilty because her dog was at home and hungry.

1:   To protect client privacy, names and details used in this book have been changed.

Step 2: Name the "Shoulds"

The second step in the process is to identify your judgments—what you're telling yourself you should or shouldn't do about the situation. Sometimes these messages will flow easily; other times you may hold back, not wanting to subject yourself to that kind of blame and attack. I encourage you to uncover all the "shoulds," even from the meanest bone in your body. After all, you are already telling yourself these things. We usually carry much more judgment unconsciously than consciously, and digging deeply into possible judgments allows us to discover what might be hidden inside. The more that is uncovered in this step, the deeper the potential for transformation and relief in the later steps.

•   •   •

We asked Jenny what she was telling herself about not feeding her dog. She told us that she shouldn't starve her dog, she shouldn't be so selfish, she shouldn't have come to class, and she should be a responsible pet owner. I wrote these four should-statements on the board.

Sometimes, you will find just three or four should-statements; other times, you may have ten, or twenty, or more. Keep writing them as long as they are flowing. If you write down a judgment that doesn't really ring true, you can cross it off your list later.

After compiling the list, read all your should-statements aloud, slowly. Usually one will feel more "charged" or tender than the others. Place a checkmark next to it for reference as you move forward.

•   •   •

I read Jenny's should-statements to her, and she decided that "I should be a responsible pet owner" felt the strongest.

Step 3: Connect With the Unmet Needs

What sets Nonviolent Communication apart from any other communication modality I've encountered is what founder Marshall Rosenberg calls *Universal Needs*. Universal Needs are the qualities that support a meaningful and fulfilling life. They include survival needs such as food, air, shelter, and safety, as well as interpersonal and spiritual needs such as connection, love, autonomy, and contribution. (Please see the starter Needs list on page 84 at the back of the book.)

When first learning NVC, some people get confused about the distinction between *needs* and *wants*. Is a cup of coffee a need or a want? What about a date with Pat? Or a new car? A clear way to differentiate needs from wants is with the question, "Does everyone on earth need this?" A friend may say that she needs a new job. Does everyone on earth need a new job? No, many people all over the globe get along quite well without any job at all. So "a new job" would be a want, not a need.

Whether something is a need or not, your desire for it is still important to acknowledge. Once you've identified a desire (a "want"), you can identify the needs behind it with one simple question. In the case of my friend and the new job, to get to the need behind the want, I would ask, "What needs would be met by her getting a new job?" Perhaps security, or appreciation, creativity, contribution, or many other needs, depending on the specifics of her situation.

I was a participant many years ago at an NVC workshop where we were discussing the subject of needs. One person asserted that only survival needs, such as safety, warmth, food and air, could be considered true needs. Another member of the group responded, "I disagree. I have cancer, and when I don't get love, connection, empathy, laughter, and creativity, I feel my life force leaving me. When I do experience those qualities in my life, I feel myself strengthening. These are not the extras of life; these needs are life itself."

In another workshop, one that I was facilitating, a woman found the word *order* on the Needs list and quickly piped up, "Order can't be a Universal Need. You should see my son's room!"

I was glad to hear this statement, because one of the key points of NVC is that while we all have the same needs, we have different ways of meeting those needs.

Earlier in the day, this woman had described how her son thrived when he had a predictable rhythm to his day and week. So I observed, "I recall that your son does his best when his day and week have a secure rhythm to them. It seems to me that he meets his need for order through having his time orderly, not his belongings."

It takes some practice to become adept at discovering needs underneath any want. Using the Needs list as a reference often helped me in my earlier days with NVC. If I couldn't think of the need on my own, I would read over the list and find that one or more Need words immediately resonated with my experience. Even after nine years of studying and teaching NVC, consulting the list still helps me pinpoint an elusive need and deepen my self-understanding.

In step 3 of the Graduating From Guilt process, you ask yourself what Needs are not being met by your actions.

• • •

> *In connecting with her unmet needs, Jenny found many needs related to interdependence, such as care, nurturing, connection, and trust. She also found that her needs for trusting herself, for accountability, and for integrity were unmet. Her dog's need for food was unmet, and Jenny's needs for peace of mind and focus were also not met, as she was worrying about the dog instead of being focused on the class.*

The number of Needs you identify will vary depending on the situation, from just a couple to nearly the whole list.

If defensiveness creeps in while you are connecting with Needs that aren't met, see if you can put the defensiveness on hold and concentrate on the needs. For example, Jenny might have thought, "Why am I blaming myself about this? My dog hasn't missed a meal in six months." Defending yourself rather than connecting with the unmet needs may lead to temporary relief, but it will not bring you the full transformation that mourning the unmet needs will. When defensive thoughts come up, refocus on the question, "What needs are not being met by my action?" (It may be helpful to bring your attention lower in the body by settling your hands on your abdominal area. In my classes, we sometimes place a small blue beanbag, one of the Centering Buddies,[2] on the abdomen to support a focus on needs.)

Step 4: Experience the Feelings of the Unmet Needs

We begin to experience the Feelings of the unmet needs simply by reading aloud the list of Needs compiled in step 3. It is important to pause for a moment after reading each need, to let its power sink in. As you connect with the unmet needs, allow your feelings to surface. You may still feel guilty. You may also notice other feelings emerging.

• • •

I read the list of unmet needs to Jenny. As I read each word, "Care, nurturing, connection, trust," she became quieter, and deepened with herself. After reading the whole list, I asked her how she felt, and she said, "I'm worried about my dog." After a pause, she added, "And sad because I know he needs me." She sat with these two feelings silently for a few moments, then her distraught demeanor returned, and she said, "And I still feel GUILTY!!"

Sit with these feelings for as long as it takes to experience them fully. This may be one minute or twenty. If you have a set of Centering Buddies, place the heart-shaped beanbag over your heart and feel the weight on your chest. If you begin to cry, let the tears flow. It is important to actually feel the feelings that come up. If the steps become just a mental exercise, you probably won't experience the actual shifts that free you from your guilt.

2:   I developed the small colored beanbags called Centering Buddies as a somatic invitation to experience Feelings and Needs more deeply. A red-velvet beanbag in the shape of the heart is placed on the chest to invite connection with feelings. A blue-velvet circle beanbag is held on the abdomen (the core) to invite connection with needs (the core motivators). You can see the Centering Buddies in action at www.HollyEckert.com.

The purpose of step 4 is to mourn—to feel the regret and sadness that is already inside you (and which might have been covered up by the guilt). In this step, you bring yourself into present time by catching up with the suppressed, unfelt emotions of the past.

Focusing on the Needs (step 3) rather than the judgment (step 2) will usually move you away from the guilt and into sadness or fear or both. However, if guilt is still a dominant feeling at this point, that's just fine. There are still several steps during which the guilt can be transformed.

Step 5: Connect With the Positive Motivations

Step 5 is the time to look at what possible positive motivations affected the choice that you made. According to NVC philosophy, every action is motivated by a beautiful need. In other words, whatever people say or do, they are trying to meet a need.

Even if someone's conscious motivation is to hurt another, if you keep going to deeper levels, you will always come to a positive motivation. Take for example a wife who leaves the family car with the fuel tank so low that the empty light is on, just so her husband will know how much she suffers when he does the same to her. Even if her conscious motivation is revenge, all we have to do is ask her the question, "When you get all the revenge that you want, then what need will be met?" I imagine that her answer might be, "Then he'll know how his actions affect me," revealing needs for empathy and understanding.

In step 5, you begin to see that your motivations were pure and that there were some very good reasons for choosing as you did (even if it ultimately resulted in some unmet needs for yourself or others). This clears the path for self-forgiveness. If you have trouble identifying your positive motivations, look once again to the Needs list.

It is often enlightening to compare the needs found in step 3 (the unmet needs) with the needs found in step 5 (the positive motivations). Notice, in the worksheet at the end of this chapter, that Jenny lists *connection* under both steps. This shows that connection is one of her biggest overall priorities in the situation. (See also the chapter on "Finding Independence.")

. . .

Jenny was worried about still feeling guilty at this
point, but I asked her to refocus on the process and
connect with why she came to the class. She said that
she was hoping for better connection and sense of
harmony with her family. She was also motivated by
wanting more freedom and integrity in her own life,
to live her life from a place of authenticity.

Noticing her positive motivations—connection,
harmony, freedom, integrity, and authenticity—gave
her some relief, but did not totally dissipate the guilt.

Step 6: Check In and Make a Request

Step 6 is a time for a check-in and action. Here is where we learn if we have graduated from our guilt. If so, we can take action from a place of clarity.

The check-in consists of the four parts of the Nonviolent Communication model.[3]

☑ **OBSERVATIONS:** Observe the action you took that stimulated the guilt in the first place. In the Graduating From Guilt process, we start with recalling what happened. For example, "I recall locking the door even after my son told me that he couldn't find the key," or "I recall telling Mary that I didn't think she was cut out for the job."

☑ **FEELINGS:** State how you feel in the present moment about what you recall doing. For example, "I feel sad and discouraged," or "I still feel guilty." Sometimes you will have already graduated from your guilt and may say, "I feel peaceful and satisfied."

3:   For more on the Nonviolent Communication model, please consult Marshall Rosenberg's *Nonviolent Communication: A Language of Life,* available from PuddleDancer Press.

☑ **NEEDS:** Connect with the Need(s) related to the Feelings just stated. For example, "I feel sad because I didn't meet my need for contribution," or "I feel satisfied that I was meeting my needs for authenticity and integrity." If your feeling is one of sadness, anger, fear, or guilt, you will be stating an unmet need. If your feeling is relief, satisfaction, or joy, you will be identifying a met need.

☑ **REQUESTS:** State what you'd like to ask yourself to do about the situation. Make sure your Request is a concrete action (Tape a note to the bathroom mirror and the front door) rather than a general goal (Try to do a better job at remembering).

• • •

Jenny started her check-in: "When I come to class, knowing my dog is at home waiting to be fed, I feel guilty because I haven't met my needs for accountability and care. See, I still feel guilty!"

"Yes, you do," I replied, "and I'm glad that you're being honest with us about it. There is still one more part to step 6. What action can you take that would better meet your needs for accountability and care?"

With a puzzled look on her face, Jenny got quiet again. After a few moments, she began to beam. "Next time I go out in the evening, I could ask my neighbor to feed my dog!" she said.

Now, any of us in the class could have suggested this solution right from the start. Jenny couldn't see any solution herself because she was caught up in her judgments and her feeling of guilt. Once she had gone through the process, she came to a deeper self-connection about the situation, and she could then make an empowering request of herself.

"How's your level of guilt now?" I asked.

Jenny was quiet for a moment as she checked in with her guilt. Then she broke into a huge grin and replied: "You know what? It is completely gone!"

Most of the time, you will feel lighter, freer, and centered within your sense of integrity after completing the six steps. In some cases, you may still feel guilty at the end of step 6. If so, return to step 2, and either pick another should-statement you have already written or brainstorm some more. Then repeat steps 3 through 6 with the new should-statement until you feel the relief and freedom of graduating from guilt.

Graduating From Guilt

Holly Michelle Eckert, CNVC Certified Trainer

Six Steps to Freedom

❶ What do you feel guilty about?

Leaving my dog at home, hungry.

❷ What are you telling yourself you should or shouldn't do?

I shouldn't starve my dog.

I shouldn't be so selfish.

I shouldn't have come to class.

✓ I should be a responsible pet owner.*

❸ What needs are not met by the choice you made?

interdependence	accountability
care	integrity
nurturing	food
connection	peace of mind
trust	focus

❹ How do you feel when you get in touch with these unmet needs?

worried

sad

guilty

*This is the statement that felt most charged or most tender to the participant.

5 What needs were you attempting to meet by the choice you made?

connection

harmony

freedom

integrity

authenticity

6 What are your Observations, Feelings, Needs, and Requests in the present moment?

O   When I come to class, knowing my dog is at home waiting to be fed,

F   I feel guilty

N   because my needs for accountability and care are not met.

R   The next time I go out in the evening, would I ask my neighbor to feed my dog?

If you still feel guilty, choose another should-statement and repeat steps 3–6.

Learning Self-Care

Let's take a look at another example from the Graduating From Guilt class. This participant felt guilty about the fact that he had needs. Universal Needs are at the heart of Nonviolent Communication, but many people grow up being told they should be selfless, generous, and charitable toward others. When these folks start learning NVC, they can feel quite guilty about having needs at all.

Step 1: Identify the Guilt

Roger was one such person. While attending the Graduating From Guilt class, he wanted to work through guilt around his new awareness that he actually had needs.

Step 2: Name the "Shoulds"

When asked to expand on the idea that he shouldn't have Needs, Roger came up with two groups of statements that seemed in opposition. The first group: "I shouldn't meet my needs at the expense of other people," "I shouldn't inconvenience or hurt others," and "I should use my talents for the good of others."

This group of needs was followed by guilt from his inner advocate, telling Roger to stick up for himself—"I should follow my bliss," and "I should be more clear and courageous about what I need and want." Just for good measure, Roger judged himself for his confusion, with "I should be able to sort through these issues more clearly."

I read Roger's list back to him, and the statement that touched him most tenderly was "I should be more clear and courageous about what I need and want."

Step 3: Connect With the Unmet Needs

I invited Roger to connect with his unmet needs by asking him, "What needs of yours are unmet when you are not clear and courageous about what you need and want?"

Roger had no problem answering. "Acceptance for my own sense of authenticity. I'm out of touch with my autonomy, creativity, self-expression, and self-empowerment. When I don't act on what I want in life, I miss out on fulfillment, joy, purpose, meaning, and direction. I really care to grow, and that need is not being met either. And if I'm not expressing myself authentically, how can anyone offer me empathy or understanding?"

Step 4: Experience the Feelings of the Unmet Needs

I captured these needs in list form and said, "I'm going to read your list back to you very slowly. I'll pause between each need so you can let each word settle into a deep place within you." We took a breath, and I continued: "Acceptance, authenticity. Autonomy, creativity, self-expression, and self-empowerment. Fulfillment, joy, purpose, meaning, and direction. Growth. Empathy and understanding. When these needs are not met, how do you feel?"

Roger replied, slowly and quietly, "Sad and tired. Also torn. Anxious and frustrated, too." We paused for a few moments so Roger could experience these feelings.

Step 5: Connect With the Positive Motivations

"Roger," I continued, "I'm quite sure that there are some beautiful needs that have kept you in the pattern of meeting other people's needs before your own. Are you ready to discover what they might be?"

"Yes, well, definitely connection. I keep a lid on my own needs because it seems an easier route to harmony, peace, and love. Not only that, but I also enjoy the nurturing and contribution when I meet other people's needs. I see that respect is somehow involved—it's like I respect others' needs, and they respect my contributions. In that way, a need for acceptance is also met. Doing what others want distracts me from taking a chance on something new, so I guess that meets my needs for safety and security."

By the end of this list, Roger seemed relaxed yet engaged.

Step 6: Check In and Make a Request

I could tell that the mourning (steps 3 and 4) and self-forgiveness (step 5) processes had worked their magic. Roger launched himself right into the final pieces in step 6—Observations, Feelings, Needs, and Requests. I wrote Roger's words on the board.

☑ **OBSERVATIONS:** "When I think about doing something, and I'm not clear if it would lead to an unmet need for the other person . . ."

☑ **FEELINGS:** "I feel anxious and torn . . ."

☑ **NEEDS:** "because I need clarity."

☑ **REQUESTS:** "Would I be willing to tell the other person my plan and check in with them, such as 'I'd like to postpone our meeting until Monday. How does that affect you?'"

"It seems so simple!" Roger concluded. "It feels really good to be able to stick up for my own needs without trampling over the needs of others."

Graduating From Guilt

Holly Michelle Eckert, CNVC Certified Trainer

Learning Self-Care

1 What do you feel guilty about?

I feel guilty for having needs.

2 What are you telling yourself you should or shouldn't do?

I shouldn't meet my needs at the expense of other people.

I shouldn't inconvenience or hurt others.

I should use my talents for the good of others.

I should follow my bliss.

✓ I should be more clear and courageous about what I need and want.

I should be able to sort through these issues more clearly.

3 What needs are not met by the choice you made?

acceptance	joy
authenticity	purpose
autonomy	meaning
creativity	direction
self-expression	growth
self-empowerment	empathy
fulfillment	understanding

4 How do you feel when you get in touch with these unmet needs?

sad   anxious
tired   frustrated
torn

5 What needs were you attempting to meet by the choice you made?

connection   contribution
harmony   respect
peace   acceptance
love   safety
nurturing   security

6 What are your Observations, Feelings, Needs, and Requests in the present moment?

O   When I think about doing something, and I'm not clear if it would lead to an unmet need for the other person,

F   I feel anxious and torn

N   because I need clarity.

R   Would I be willing to tell the other person my plan and check in with them, such as "I'd like to postpone our meeting until Monday. How does that affect you?"

If you still feel guilty, choose another should-statement and repeat steps 3–6.

Healing From Regret

Family relationships can be a hotbed of guilt. At least half of the situations that Graduating From Guilt participants bring into the class (and several of the examples in this book) are related to family relationships. The most common scenario is the guilty parent.

Step 1: Identify the Guilt

Mary Beth came to the Graduating From Guilt class with decades of unresolved guilt. A middle-aged recovering alcoholic, she had deep-seated guilt around not being more present (physically and emotionally) for her son, John, when he was growing up.

Step 2: Name the "Shoulds"

Mary Beth's should-statements were concise and direct. She said that she should have spent more time with John one-on-one, especially since he was an only child. She should have protected him from two (or possibly more) abusive relatives. She should have paid attention to the signs of John's distress.

All three of these statements were equally alive for Mary Beth, so we moved forward holding all three in our awareness.

Step 3: Connect With the Unmet Needs

Even though there were only three should-statements, we found many more unmet needs. The first unmet need was communication. Mary

Beth missed the opportunity to talk about thoughts, feelings, and ideas with her son. When she was not as present with John as she would like, Mary Beth's needs for love, intimacy, and warmth went unmet. And because her actions were not aligned with her values, Mary Beth's need for integrity was not met. Several other needs for contribution remained unfulfilled—Mary Beth wanted to offer protection, understanding, support, and consideration to her child. Lastly, Mary Beth's self-worth was called into question, since she wanted to be competent as a mother.

Step 4: Experience the Feelings of the Unmet Needs

I read back the list of unmet needs to Mary Beth and asked her to close her eyes and sink into her Feelings. Once she settled into herself, she expressed feeling tremendously regretful, sorrowful, and lonely. We paused for a few moments to honor those feelings.

Step 5: Connect With the Positive Motivations

When I sensed that Mary Beth was ready to proceed, I reminded her that all actions originally have some positive motivation. I asked her if she could connect with any Needs that she might have been trying to meet with the choices she made.

"Yes," she responded. "I didn't know how to handle my own pain, so I turned to drinking. It gave me protection, safety, and space. In concentrating on my own needs, I also got a sense of security, order, and control. When my life and my relationship with John felt chaotic and unmanageable, escaping into my own world—either through drinking or just pursuing my own projects—gave me a much-needed sense of peace."

I sensed that Mary Beth was centered in both the unmet needs and the needs she had been attempting to meet, so we moved into the final step of the process.

Step 6: Check In and Make a Request

At this point, Mary Beth expressed her Observations, Feelings, Needs, and Requests in the present moment.

☑ **OBSERVATIONS:** "When I recall pursuing my own projects instead of talking with John . . ."

☑ **FEELINGS:** "I feel desolate and bereft."

☑ **NEEDS:** "I need to be trusted and to be accountable, so . . ."

☑ **REQUESTS:** "would I be willing to invite John into conversation about this?"

Mary Beth considered her request for a moment, then said: "After all these years, I am ready. I am ready to hear John's pain and to be present to it in a way that I've never been able to before. I can't undo the past, but I've come to terms with it in myself and am ready to heal the relationship between us. Our disconnection has gone on long enough."

Graduating From Guilt

Holly Michelle Eckert, CNVC Certified Trainer

Healing From Regret

1 What do you feel guilty about?

Not being more present for John when he was growing up.

2 What are you telling yourself you should or shouldn't do?

✓ I should have spent more time with him one-on-one.

✓ I should have protected him from abusive relatives.

✓ I should have paid attention to the signs of his distress.

3 What needs are not met by the choice you made?

communication	protection
love	understanding
intimacy	support
warmth	consideration
integrity	self-worth

4 How do you feel when you get in touch with these unmet needs?

tremendously regretful

sorrowful

lonely

5 What needs were you attempting to meet by the choice you made?

protection

safety

space

security

order

control

peace

6 What are your Observations, Feelings, Needs, and Requests in the present moment?

O When I recall pursuing my own projects instead of talking with John,

F I feel desolate and bereft.

N I need to be trusted and to be accountable, so

R would I be willing to invite John into conversation about this?

If you still feel guilty, choose another should-statement and repeat steps 3–6.

Reconciling at a Distance

Ingrid came to my office for a Graduating From Guilt private session. Ingrid had moved to the Pacific Northwest from the East Coast some years before, while her mother and brothers still lived in Boston. Ingrid described a tumultuous relationship with her mother, Anna, including many periods of silence between the two of them.

Anna had died about five years before Ingrid's session with me. About a year before her death, while living in a nursing home, Anna had expressed unhappiness about her doctor to Ingrid. Ingrid arranged for a new doctor to care for Anna—especially to help her in managing pain. Briefing the doctor on her mother's medical history, Ingrid told the doctor that they had never had a very happy family life.

Step 1: Identify the Guilt

When I asked Ingrid to pinpoint what she felt most guilty about, she said she felt guilty about telling Anna's doctor difficult truths about their family. Ingrid also felt guilty about forcing the new doctor on her mother, when her mother didn't want a new doctor at all.

Step 2: Name the "Shoulds"

I asked Ingrid if she could share some of the thoughts she had in her mind regarding what she should or shouldn't have done.

"Well, part of me says that I shouldn't have told the truth. I shouldn't even see the family through this dark lens.

"Hmm, something also about loyalty. I shouldn't share intimate family things outside the family. I shouldn't be disloyal. I shouldn't publicly wash our family's dirty laundry. What seems the strongest for me is that I shouldn't be disloyal to my family."

Step 3: Connect With the Unmet Needs

"Thank you, Ingrid," I replied. "So what needs are not met when you are not more loyal to your family?"

"My need to have my integrity recognized wasn't met. I was trying to give the new doctor the information she needed to give my mother the best care, and no one saw that intention—in fact, my brother criticized my decision," she said. "Nor did my actions contribute to my mother's sense of empowerment, and for that I feel very sad."

"What about a sense of belonging with the family? Did this cause a divide?" I wondered.

"Well, I haven't had a sense of belonging with the family for eons," Ingrid sighed, "and this was just one more example of us not working together. . . .

"I also have a need to know that I did the right thing—to be effective, you might say," she finished.

Step 4: Experience the Feelings of the Unmet Needs

After checking in with Ingrid to see if there were any more unmet needs, I read the list to her and asked her how she felt. She placed her hands over her heart, closed her eyes, and replied, "Sad, and lonely, too."

We stayed with those feelings for a minute or so before moving on.

Step 5: Connect With the Positive Motivations

"Ready to go on?" I asked. Ingrid nodded, and I continued. "What would you say motivated you to tell your information to the new doctor?"

"All I wanted to do was to get my mother the best possible care. I thought that with more information, the doctor would be better prepared to help her," Ingrid said.

"Sounds like needs for contribution and care," I suggested.

"Yes, that's right, and support! Not only did I want to support my mother, I also wanted support for myself. Being across the country from my mother, I wanted to be well connected with her doctor so that we could have an accurate information exchange. I thought that communicating transparently with the doctor would give me a sense of ease and trust.

"But, honestly, most of all, I wanted my mother to have some help in managing her pain so she could live with as much peace as possible," Ingrid concluded. We sat quietly for a moment with Ingrid's positive intention.

Step 6: Check In and Make a Request

"OK, let's see where we are," I suggested. "Think back on talking to the doctor, and let's list your Observations, Feelings, Needs, and Requests in this present moment."

☑ **OBSERVATIONS:** "When I recall telling the doctor about our disharmonious family . . ."

☑ **FEELINGS:** "I feel content . . ."

☑ **NEEDS:** "because now that I review the whole story, I see that I did meet my need for integrity."

"I have other feelings, though, too," she offered.

"That's fine," I said, "let's do another Feeling and Need round."

☑ **FEELINGS:** "I also feel lonely and sad . . ."

☑ **NEEDS:** "because of a longtime unmet need for connection. The last moments I saw my mother, a few months before her death, she was just as happy to turn on the TV as to connect with me."

"Yes," I said, "I can see how you would feel lonely and sad."

After a pause to acknowledge those feelings, I continued. "We can come back to your feelings in a minute if you want. How about we finish with the request and then see where we want to go next?"

☑ **REQUESTS:** "Sure. I request of myself to just drop it!" she exclaimed.

"Wanting to drop it is just fine. How specifically might you do that? What action would you take?" I asked.

"It's too bad that I'm not a practicing Catholic any more—a confession and absolution seems in order," Ingrid said.

"Could there be a similar action that would result in the same feeling of forgiveness for you?" I wondered.

☑ **REQUESTS:** "I suppose that one option would be to write a letter to Mom, expressing honestly the things I said that I now see resulted in unmet needs for both of us. I could also explain to her the reasons for my words and actions. That might give me the peace I'm looking for."

"Great," I said. "Now you have an action that could bring you the relief you've been wanting for many years. Knowing that you have that option, how are you doing right now?" I asked.

"I feel pretty good, actually. I feel relieved about having done the right thing. I'm no longer judging myself for being mean," she concluded, face softened.

Graduating From Guilt

Holly Michelle Eckert, CNVC Certified Trainer

Reconciling at a Distance

1 What do you feel guilty about?

Telling my mother's new doctor some difficult truths about our family.

Forcing my mother to switch to a new doctor.

2 What are you telling yourself you should or shouldn't do?

I shouldn't have told the truth.

I shouldn't see our family through this dark lens.

I shouldn't share intimate family things outside the family.

✓ I shouldn't be disloyal.

I shouldn't publicly wash our family's dirty laundry.

3 What needs are not met by the choice you made?

recognition of my integrity

empowerment

belonging

effectiveness

4 How do you feel when you get in touch with these unmet needs?

sad

lonely

5 What needs were you attempting to meet by the choice you made?

contribution

care

support

ease

trust

peace

6 What are your Observations, Feelings, Needs, and Requests in the present moment?

O   When I recall telling the doctor about our disharmonious family,

F   I feel content

N   because I did meet my need for integrity.

F   I also feel lonely and sad

N   because my need for connection wasn't met.

R   I request of myself to write a letter to Mom, expressing honestly the things I said that I now see resulted in unmet needs for both of us. I could also explain to her the reasons for my words and actions.

If you still feel guilty, choose another should-statement and repeat steps 3–6.

Mastering the Process

You will find it is possible to use the six-step process and feel relief before reaching step 6. Connecting with the positive motivation needs in step 5 will at times set the guilt free. When this happens, feelings such as calm, content, or satisfied will be affirmed in step 6.

I once taught the Graduating From Guilt class immediately after moving in to a new teaching location. The new location was tucked away on a side street, and the front door was hidden under a twelve-foot-long breezeway. Several of the participants came in late, flustered and confused, because they hadn't known how to find the class. As participants entered in a state of stress, it became clear to me that my own sense of guilt was irrepressibly alive. I used my own guilt to demonstrate the Graduating From Guilt process to the class.

Step 1: Identify the Guilt

I identified the stimulus of my guilt as "I feel guilty for not being more considerate of tonight's participants."

Step 2: Name the "Shoulds"

My mind was spinning with everything I should have done to prevent the confusion. "I should have made reminder calls to all of you, giving you specifics about the location," I told the class. "I definitely should have a clear sign. I should have e-mailed you directions, or at the very least, I should have a page on my Web site where you can access the information. I'm telling myself that I should support you in having clarity and ease in your class experience, including in getting here." All the previous should-statements led me to the one that I held dearest— that I should support participants in having clarity and ease in their class experience.

Step 3: Connect With the Unmet Needs

When I asked myself what Needs went unmet in this situation, when participants did not experience clarity and ease, the first need that jumped to my mind was consideration. I saw that I hadn't provided the clarity or ease that leads to security. I started to imagine participants getting annoyed and not wanting to come back for future classes and realized that my need for sustainability, especially considering my new lease payments, was unmet. Even deeper than that, without students, I couldn't teach, so my sense of meaning and purpose in life felt vulnerable. Lastly, I thought of how I would miss the connection and learning I usually get in teaching a class. This led me right into the feelings of the unmet needs.

Step 4: Experience the Feelings of the Unmet Needs

"Without any of you here to help me meet these needs for connection and learning, I feel lonely and sad," I told the class. "I feel discouraged about not having contributed more to your ease and clarity. When I focus on my unmet needs for sustainability and purpose, I get pretty anxious." I asked the class if they would sit with me in silence for a bit while the feelings grew, crested, then started to wane.

Step 5: Connect With the Positive Motivations

In looking for positive motivations, or the needs that I was attempting to meet, I had to ask myself why I hadn't created a sign or sent out an e-mail. I immediately remembered that I had been waiting a few days to print a sign until a professional artist could design one for me. Instead of making a sign that would be used for only a few days and then be replaced, I was meeting my need for efficiency. I was also meeting my need for beauty by waiting for the professionally made sign.

There had been so much to do to prepare the room for the class that until the last day, my colleagues, friends, and I were patching holes in walls, painting, sewing curtains, repotting plants, and building furniture. We made those choices so we would have the beauty, peace, and inspiration of a lovely room during the class.

During that last day before the evening class, I also met with a couple in crisis as well as another individual for a private appointment. These meetings were motivated by practical concerns (paying the rent) as well as spiritual needs—for support, contribution, and meaning.

When I stepped back and looked at the needs I had met by how I chose to spend my time, a wave of self-forgiveness washed over me. The idea that I should have done anything different with my time was completely gone.

Step 6: Check In and Make a Request

With lightheartedness, I flowed into the final Observations, Feelings, Needs, and Requests.

- ☑ **OBSERVATIONS:** "When I see that I didn't distribute directions to this class or make a sign . . ."

- ☑ **FEELINGS:** "I feel calm and content . . ."

- ☑ **NEEDS:** "because I met my need for integrity, acting in alignment with my priorities."

- ☑ **REQUESTS:** "In order to further contribute to clarity and ease for future participants, would I (1) ask my office assistant to call future participants with the directions, and (2) ask her to put the location and directions on my Web site?"

I wrote down those two requests in my assistant's task notebook. Through the Graduating From Guilt process, I connected with my regrets and made space for my self-appreciation to enter. As a result, I felt completely centered and present to teach the rest of the class.

Graduating From Guilt

Holly Michelle Eckert, CNVC Certified Trainer

Mastering the Process

1 What do you feel guilty about?

Not being more considerate of tonight's participants.

2 What are you telling yourself you should or shouldn't do?

I should have made reminder calls, giving specifics about the location.

I should have a clear sign.

I should have e-mailed directions.

I should have directions on my Web site.

✓ I should support participants' having clarity and ease.

3 What needs are not met by the choice you made?

consideration   meaning

clarity   purpose

ease   connection

security   learning

sustainability

4 How do you feel when you get in touch with these unmet needs?

lonely   discouraged

sad   anxious

5 What needs were you attempting to meet by the choice you
made?

efficiency   sustainability
beauty   support
peace   contribution
inspiration   meaning

6 What are your Observations, Feelings, Needs, and Requests in
the present moment?

O   When I see that I didn't distribute
     directions to this class or make a sign,

F   I feel calm and content

N   because I met my need for integrity, acting
     in alignment with my priorities.

R   In order to further contribute to clarity and
     ease for future participants, would I (1) ask
     my office assistant to call future
     participants with the directions, and (2) ask
     her to put the location and directions on my
     Web site?

If you still feel guilty, choose another should-statement and repeat
steps 3–6.

Forgiving Yourself

As we've seen, the Graduating From Guilt process supports transformation in situations of specific acts, such as leaving a hungry dog at home or revealing family information to a doctor. It also supports people working through guilt over more generalized or broader-ranging situations.

In my home, the Pacific Northwest of the United States, eco-consciousness is a common mind-set. People are concerned about rainforest destruction, energy consumption, and waste of any kind. One woman in her forties, Rebecca, came to the Graduating From Guilt class in a cloud of guilt about using resources.

Step 1: Identify the Guilt

I asked Rebecca to distill the problem into an opening sentence. "That's just impossible. There are so many things that I feel guilty about," she said.

"We can get to all the different specifics in the next step," I replied. "Is there one blanket statement that can cover all, or even most of them?"

Rebecca thought for a moment and answered, "I suppose that 'I feel guilty for being so wasteful' would apply to most of the specifics."

"Great. Let's start there—feeling guilty for being so wasteful. Let's go right ahead to the specifics."

Step 2: Name the "Shoulds"

"What are you telling yourself you should or shouldn't do?" I asked. "I'm ready to write your should-statements up on the board."

"How much time do we have?" she joked. Then Rebecca settled into her judgments of herself, and they started to roll off her tongue with great ease. "First of all, I shouldn't live in such a big house. There are only two of us—why can't we get something more efficient? And if I'm going to have such a big house, I shouldn't turn the heat up so high. Maybe I should explore alternative power sources for my home.

"I have a lot of 'shoulds' around food. I definitely shouldn't eat food transported to Seattle from elsewhere. I should support the local economy at the farmers' market or even grow my own garden.

"I should be using my money to help others more. How can I justify a new sweater when people all over the world are starving and have no water or sanitation?

"Oh yes, then there is transportation. I should never fly on airplanes. Also, I shouldn't drive so much. I really should be more efficient."

Rebecca paused for a moment. The pressure had finally blown the lid off the pot, and now that the steam was pouring out, we could begin to see the contents. "What else are you settling into?" I asked.

Thoughtfully and quietly, she replied, "At the core of all of this, I should do everything I can to help the planet and those on it."

I wrote this last should-statement on the board and added a checkmark, as it was clearly at the heart of the matter for Rebecca.

Step 3: Connect With the Unmet Needs

"Rebecca, when you don't do everything you can to help the planet and those on it, what needs of yours are unmet?" I asked.

"Contribution, definitely," she replied. "Food, shelter, water, even survival for people all over the place. And survival for all the plants and animals as well. When I don't do everything I can, I am out of touch with my sense of empathy and compassion for others. And when I'm disconnected from empathy and compassion, I am disconnected from my integrity—I'm not being the person in the world that I know I can be. I'm also missing being part of a larger community, awareness about being in connection with everyone here, and even a spiritual connection."

By the last sentence, Rebecca was touching into some deeply held values. I read the list I had culled from her words back to her. I gave plenty of space around the last few needs—integrity, community, planetary connection, spiritual connection.

Step 4: Experience the Feelings of the Unmet Needs

"Rebecca, what do you feel when you focus your attention on these unmet needs?" I asked.

With her eyes closed, she answered, "Somewhat worried. Also lonely, sad, and even hopeless." She started to cry a bit, releasing some of the emotion. "I feel a great longing for these things," she added.

Step 5: Connect With the Positive Motivations

After a few moments, Rebecca opened her eyes, signaling her readiness to proceed.

"Let's look at the positive motivations behind your choices," I proposed. "What is motivating you to live in your house, eat oranges, keep some money for yourself, and use airplanes and cars?"

"I love my house—it is an oasis for me. Having my house meets needs for safety, beauty, and peace. When I have that peace, I have inspiration, which unlocks my creativity. Wow—that feels good!"

"Yes, those are some beautiful needs," I replied. "And what else?"

Rebecca continued, "Well, sometimes I eat food from other parts of the country for the pleasure of it, a need for appreciation maybe? But also for the nutritional value. Try to get a good dose of vitamin C from a Seattle farmers' market in February. Good luck!" she laughed. "OK, what need would that be? Health, I guess. Yes, health, and also nurturing myself.

"Nurturing myself must also play into using money for myself. Let me tell you, I am not eating out at five-star restaurants every night! I would say that an occasional treat for myself meets a need for fun, and balance as well. Oh yes, I want to balance my own needs with the world's needs."

"We're compiling quite a list here," I remarked. "Any more needs, maybe around your transportation?"

By now, Rebecca's state of mind had already changed to acceptance. "Oh yes. I use airplanes and cars because I want connection with my loved ones. I also want a certain degree of efficiency in getting where I need to go so I can make a difference in the world. You see, what I do for a living is raise people's awareness about global issues. What I was judging myself for not doing, I actually do every day—I am contributing in a major way! And I want to raise awareness that you don't have to be an ascetic to make a difference."

Step 6: Check In and Make a Request

"Rebecca, it sounds like you have already graduated from your guilt. Would you like to complete step 6 to see if there is anything additional that you'd like to ask of yourself?" I inquired.

"I feel much lighter already, but let's go ahead," she replied.

☑ **OBSERVATIONS:** "When I recall feeling guilty for being so wasteful . . ."

☑ **FEELINGS:** "I feel amused . . ."

☑ **NEEDS:** "because I now have appreciation for all the contributions I do make."

Rebecca was stumped on the request part of the model. "What request can there possibly be?" she wondered.

I asked her if she thought that she might ever fall into guilt and judgment of herself again. "Oh yes. But only about ten times a day," she said with a smile.

"What if we make a request that will help you live in the place you want to be when that guilt comes knocking at your door again?" I suggested. "You could make yourself a little card to keep in your pocket with your pure intention. Perhaps it might say something like

'I contribute in balance.' Then whenever you need a reminder of your deepest intentions, you could pull it out and remind yourself. Can you think of a phrase you'd like to use to remind yourself?"

"I get your drift," Rebecca replied. "Here's my request—

☑ **REQUEST:** "I'd like to request that I write 'Name three contributions you've made today' on my pocket card. That will get me out of self-judgment and into self-appreciation. Then I can make a decision out of gratitude rather than fear."

"You have just stumbled upon one of the most life-enhancing benefits of Nonviolent Communication," I affirmed. "Rather than taking action out of fear of rejection or punishment, even punishment that comes from yourself, you can take action through your values and intentions by connecting with your needs. In this case, instead of acting from a place of judgment, you are acting from a place of balance and contribution, and it is clear that you feel the difference."

Graduating From Guilt

Holly Michelle Eckert, CNVC Certified Trainer

Forgiving Yourself

1 What do you feel guilty about?

Being so wasteful.

2 What are you telling yourself you should or shouldn't do?

I shouldn't live in such a big house.

I shouldn't turn up the heat so high.

I should explore alternative power sources for my home.

I shouldn't eat transported food.

I should shop at the farmers' market.

I should grow my own garden.

I should use my money to help others.

I shouldn't fly on airplanes.

I shouldn't drive so much.

I should be more efficient.

✓ I should do everything I can to help the planet and those on it.

3 What needs are not met by the choice you made?

contribution	compassion
food	integrity
shelter	community
water	connection
survival	spiritual connection
empathy	

4 How do you feel when you get in touch with these unmet needs?

worried   sad

lonely   hopeless

5 What needs were you attempting to meet by the choice you made?

safety   nurturing

beauty   fun

peace   balance

inspiration   connection

creativity   efficiency

appreciation   contribution

health

6 What are your Observations, Feelings, Needs, and Requests in the present moment?

O   When I recall feeling guilty for being so wasteful,

F   I feel amused

N   because I now have appreciation for all the contributions I do make.

R   I'm going to keep a card in my pocket saying "Name three contributions you've made today."

If you still feel guilty, choose another should-statement and repeat steps 3–6.

Gaining Perspective

One of the things that I appreciate about the Graduating From Guilt process (as well as NVC in general) is that it works in any situation—from situations with deep-seated guilt that drains energy almost constantly to milder situations where guilt may be only a fleeting thought.

I was compiling the examples for this book when my sister sent me an instant message asking to chat online. As I wanted to move forward on the book but also wanted to connect with my sister, I asked, somewhat in jest, if she felt guilty about anything. Surprisingly enough, she said, "Yes, actually I do."

Step 1: Identify the Guilt

My sister, Em, said that she felt guilty for getting a new kitten when they already had two cats in the house.

Step 2: Name the "Shoulds"

Em's judgments about her situation were pretty direct. She said that she shouldn't be so selfish about doing what she wanted, and that she shouldn't do things to upset the older cats.

Step 3: Connect With the Unmet Needs

When she said that she shouldn't upset the older cats, I asked her if she had unmet needs around consideration and respect of the older cats. "Yes," she said, "I want the old ladies to be comfortable with their status in the house."

"The three of them may not ever get along very well," she added, to which I responded, "Sounds like you're not getting the harmony or peace that you would like."

"Yes, and, the older cats were used to me doting all over them. Now they don't get nearly as much attention," she said.

"Right," I said, "You sound sad about unmet needs for attention and love."

Step 4: Experience the Feelings of the Unmet Needs

I read Em the list of her unmet needs and asked her how she felt. "Mostly sad," she answered, "but stressed and worried as well. There may always be tension between them."

Step 5: Connect With the Positive Motivations

After a moment's pause, I asked her, "What were some of the positive motivations behind getting the kitten?"

Her voice became animated as she started listing them off. "Fun, for sure! I thought that the older cats might enjoy having a spicy little playmate. I also thought that they would like to have the chance to take care of a wee one."

"Mmm," I replied, "a need for nurturing."

"I also wanted the kitten so I could have my own cat, too," she continued. She had just moved from Seattle to Western Australia to live with her husband, who had had the two older cats for many years. I asked her, "Do you think having your own cat would give you a sense of belonging?"

"Yeah, maybe so," she replied. "I hoped that the kitten would always be my personal buddy."

"I bet some reliable friendship and companionship would feel nice when you're in a new place and hardly know anybody," I offered.

"I know what else—I also thought that it would be easier to integrate a new cat if it was younger. Oh," she said urgently, "and if I didn't take the kitten, they might have just put her down."

"Wow," I said, "the need to contribute to another being's survival is pretty compelling, isn't it?"

Step 6: Check In and Make a Request

"Let's check in and see if anything has happened as a result of this exercise," I suggested. "When you think about having gotten your kitten, how do you feel?"

☑ **OBSERVATIONS:** "When I think about having gotten my kitten . . ."

☑ **FEELINGS:** "I actually feel pretty happy about all the flavor she brings to the house . . ."

☑ **NEEDS:** "because she meets my needs for fun, play, learning, companionship, and most of all, entertainment."

"Sounds like a nice transformation," I said. "And what would you like to request of yourself about this?"

☑ **REQUESTS:** "Whenever I get worried about the cats not getting along, I want to remind myself that things are smoothing themselves out," she finished.

At this point, I could have asked her to take a more concrete action, such as putting up a sign that says, "Take a breath, things are getting better—integration and harmony are on their way." Sometimes concrete actions are helpful and even necessary to follow through on positive intentions. However, in this case, Em seemed to be well-grounded in trust that improvements were already happening, and I didn't want to get caught up in strategizing toward a need that no longer seemed to be unmet.

Graduating From Guilt

Holly Michelle Eckert, CNVC Certified Trainer

Gaining Perspective

1 What do you feel guilty about?

For getting a new kitten when there were already two cats in the house.

2 What are you telling yourself you should or shouldn't do?

I shouldn't be selfish about doing what I want.

I shouldn't do things that upset the older cats.

3 What needs are not met by the choice you made?

consideration   peace

respect   attention

comfort   love

harmony

4 How do you feel when you get in touch with these unmet needs?

sad

stressed

worried

5 What needs were you attempting to meet by the choice you made?

fun and play	companionship
nurturing	ease
belonging	contribution
friendship	survival

6 What are your Observations, Feelings, Needs, and Requests in the present moment?

O When I think about having gotten my new kitten,

F I feel pretty happy about all the flavor she brings to the house,

N because she meets my needs for fun, play, learning, companionship, and entertainment.

R I want to remind myself that things are smoothing themselves out.

If you still feel guilty, choose another should-statement and repeat steps 3–6.

Transforming Relationships

If you notice a recurring pattern of guilt-inducing behavior in your life, it can be helpful to take one specific instance of it through the Graduating From Guilt process. For example, one client of mine, Joseph, said that he felt guilty for reacting to stressful situations by "bolting," time and time again. When things got heated, he would emotionally and even physically remove himself from relationships. I asked him if he would take one specific situation through the Graduating From Guilt process. This is the situation he described:

Joseph's sister, Emma, and her two daughters, nine and fourteen years old, came to visit him in Seattle from across the country. Joseph planned a weekend excursion to Vancouver, British Columbia, a two-and-a-half-hour drive away. That Friday, Joseph received an alarming phone call from his doctor: He had a serious heart condition, was in imminent danger of a heart attack, and needed to begin medication immediately. Panicked and confused, Joseph started on the medication, then went ahead with the weekend plans. Rather than finding rest and connection in the trip, though, Joseph experienced more stress. First, they stopped several times during the drive to accommodate the younger niece's food desires. Joseph, wanting to be gracious despite thinking his nieces spoiled and overindulged, kept his annoyance to himself.

Next, Joseph had planned a family breakfast in the hotel dining room Saturday morning. When he arrived that morning, however, Emma announced that she was going to take the girls to a fast-food restaurant instead. Joseph, at his wits' end, muttered an obscenity, tossed his keys over his shoulder, and walked out the door. He wandered the city for the day, then took a bus back to Seattle. He didn't call Emma to tell her where he was and didn't speak to her for a year after the incident.

Step 1: Identify the Guilt

I asked Joseph which part of the situation he felt guilty about.

"A few things, I guess," he replied. "First of all, betraying the trust that my nieces had in me as an adult role model—ouch. I also feel guilty for leaving them there in the hotel, though probably the worst part is that I didn't approach Emma or the girls for a whole year."

Step 2: Name the "Shoulds"

I led Joseph into the next step. "Joseph, what are the things you're telling yourself that you should or shouldn't have done?"

"Oh, many things. I should have held myself together. I should have been the adult. I should have stayed in the role of playing along with our family dynamic." He searched his thoughts again with closed eyes. "I should have been clearer about asking for help in a crisis. What was I doing entertaining right after being informed of a life-threatening illness? Luckily it turned out to be a false alarm, but I didn't know that at the time. Maybe I shouldn't have gone on the trip."

He sighed. "Really, though, what I feel worst about is not resolving it sooner. I should have started talking to them much more quickly—if not before they went back to Florida, then at least well before a year's time."

As Joseph had just identified for himself that the last statement induced the most guilt, we went ahead into step 3.

Step 3: Connect With the Unmet Needs

"What needs of yours went unmet in not connecting with Emma and her girls for that year?" I asked him.

"Needs for family, love, closeness, and intimacy. A need for honesty wasn't met. Neither was authenticity. My need for forgiveness wasn't met—I think that forgiveness is part of compassion. I wanted to be loved and accepted for who I was, and I certainly didn't get that in the silence. Needs for honesty and communication are big ones for me—both listening and being heard." Joseph got quiet.

"Did you have an unmet need for peace during that time?" I wondered.

"That's right, inner peace. I was always telling myself either that I should get in touch with them or that Emma should get in touch with me. I definitely wasn't feeling peaceful about it," he answered.

Step 4: Experience the Feelings of the Unmet Needs

I asked Joseph to listen to me read his list of unmet needs and then to connect with his feelings. "Sad and hopeless. Am I ever going to have those needs met?" he said quietly.

Step 5: Connect With the Positive Motivations

"How about we see which needs might have been motivating you to avoid Emma for a year?" I offered.

"Sure, that's easy," he replied. "I was protecting myself. I wanted to avoid another confrontation—a need for harmony. And I didn't want to be judged."

"I usually translate 'not wanting to be judged' as a need for acceptance. Does that resonate with you?" I asked.

"Yes, acceptance and to be forgiven. What stopped me is that I wanted an apology from Emma, so I didn't want to make the first move," he explained.

"It sounds to me that you might have wanted some empathy in the situation," I suggested.

"Yes," he replied, nodding his head. "I certainly wanted Emma to see things from my perspective—how stressed I was—especially with the medical false alarm. I needed to receive some support, but they kept asking me to give support instead.

"You know, our whole relationship had always been full of my overfunctioning, inauthenticity, and repressed feelings of irritation and frustration," he said wistfully.

"I hear your desire for freedom from those roles and a mutual accountability," I said.

"Yes, being in crisis overwhelmed my ability to play that game any longer."

Step 6: Check In and Make a Request

I suggested that Joseph check in with himself in the present moment with regard to not contacting Emma for a year.

☑ **OBSERVATIONS:** "When I recall not having talked to Emma for a year after leaving them at the hotel . . ."

☑ **FEELINGS:** "I feel kind of neutral, actually . . ."

☑ **NEEDS:** "because I accept that it happened."

☑ **FEELINGS:** "I also feel some disappointment, regret, and guilt, not so much for me, but for my nieces . . ."

☑ **NEEDS:** "because I wanted to give them the experience of compassion and to be aligned with my integrity," he concluded.

"Is there any way that you could realign with your integrity and contribute some compassion to these girls now?" I prompted.

☑ **REQUESTS:** "Yes, I want to continue to invest in the relationships, and I'd like to find a way to use this experience as an asset—to stimulate conversation about who we are and why we make the choices that we do. This situation could serve as a cleansing fire if we let it."

"That is a beautiful intention, to continue to build the relationships. In making a request, though, you might want to choose a specific action. What are you actually going to write on your to-do list that shows your commitment to the relationships?" I asked.

☑ **REQUESTS:** "I know just what I want to do. I've thought of it in the past, and I'm ready to start acting on it. I want to begin to correspond with my nieces, send them written cards, notes, and photographs as a way of giving them some nurturing. Not just a quick e-mail, but something that they will hold in their hands and feel the love and time I put into preparing it for them."

"Planning to take that action really diminishes my feeling of guilt. I had been searching for a way to set right the bad karma and be accountable," he said. He was talking noticeably more slowly than when we had begun our conversation.

"Would you check in with your feelings one last time?" I requested.

Joseph closed his eyes and smiled. "I feel relaxed, calm, and a little lighter. Thank you."

Graduating From Guilt

Holly Michelle Eckert, CNVC Certified Trainer

Transforming Relationships

1 What do you feel guilty about?

Betraying my nieces' trust, leaving them in the hotel, and not contacting Emma for a whole year.

2 What are you telling yourself you should or shouldn't do?

I should have held myself together.

I should have been the adult.

I should have stayed in my family role.

I should have asked for help.

I shouldn't have gone on the trip.

I should have talked to them before they went back to Florida.

✓ I should have talked to them long before a year after the incident.

3 What needs are not met by the choice you made?

love	compassion
closeness	acceptance
intimacy	honesty
honesty	communication
authenticity	peace

4   How do you feel when you get in touch with these unmet needs?

sad

hopeless

5   What needs were you attempting to meet by the choice you made?

protection	support
harmony	freedom
acceptance	mutual accountability
empathy	

6   What are your Observations, Feelings, Needs, and Requests in the present moment?

O   When I recall not having talked to Emma for a year after leaving them at the hotel,

F   I feel kind of neutral

N   because I accept that it happened.

F   I also feel some disappointment, regret, and guilt

N   because I have needs for compassion and integrity.

R   To that end, I am going to send my nieces handwritten cards and photos once a month for connection and nurturing.

If you still feel guilty, choose another should-statement and repeat steps 3–6.

Finding Independence

This example demonstrates that just because a need motivates an action doesn't mean that the action always satisfies the need. In Brian's case, his strongest unmet need was also one of the original motivators.

Brian entered my office shaking his head in exasperation. "Karen just sent me a text message that said, 'I miss you.' How am I supposed to respond to that?"

Brian and Karen had been dating for a few months, until Brian broke it off about a month before our appointment. A few days before the appointment, they met to return each other's personal items and ended up sitting down for coffee, chatting, and having a playful and fun conversation.

"Yes, we had a good time together when we met up last weekend, but I have absolutely no desire to get back in the relationship. I don't want to be nice to somebody when it will increase their desire for a situation that's clearly not going to happen!" he told me. "Perhaps I should have just left her stuff on her porch."

Step 1: Identify the Guilt

"Brian, let's see if we can zero in on what you actually feel guilty about. Do you feel guilty for being nice to her over the weekend?" I asked.

"No, I feel fine about that. I guess I feel guilty for having started a relationship with her. We were two grown-ups who were going to try dating; I just didn't know how much it would end up hurting her," he replied.

Step 2: Name the "Shoulds"

"Gotcha," I said, "so are you telling yourself that you shouldn't have started the relationship at all?"

"Yup, that's it. I shouldn't have started the whole thing in the beginning. I shouldn't have led her on. When I had my knee surgery during the summer, I should have told her that I didn't need her help. I shouldn't have accepted her help. Once a woman takes care of you, it's all over," he said, shaking his head.

"At the time we met, I had a lot of stress around women. It had only been a couple of months since I had left the relationship I was in before the one with Karen. I was definitely not ready for a new relationship. Karen was just so steady and solid, with a good job and a spiritual life—I was definitely attracted to having a stabilizing influence. But I should have known better! I should have been more honest with myself that the time was not right. And I should have protected her from my own confusion.

"You know, I'm also saying that I should have been as attracted to her as she was to me. That would have made everything so much easier. She had a lot of things that I wanted, but the passion was not there. Again, I should have been more honest with myself," he concluded.

I read Brian's list to him and asked him which triggered the strongest feelings in him.

"Two of them, actually—I should have been more honest with myself, and I shouldn't have started the whole thing in the beginning," he said.

Step 3: Connect With the Unmet Needs

"OK, good, let's move into what needs of yours are now unmet because of how things actually happened," I suggested.

"Integrity. Integrity, integrity. But that just hurts, because I was acting with integrity the best way I knew how. Still, it seems that I acted inappropriately and maybe even immorally.

"I just want to be a normal human being who can have a normal long-term relationship," Brian said.

"Sure, what would that give you?" I wondered.

"Community, ease, and peace. I just want the satisfaction and fulfillment it seems most other people have," he said.

Brian continued: "Well, obviously I didn't have the honesty that I would have liked, and now I have a huge mess. I don't know how to deal with it, and I don't even feel like dealing with it! My need for clarity is definitely not met."

"I'm wondering if you need some support?" I asked.

"Maybe," he replied.

"Or empathy?" I wondered.

"Oh, yes. My friends tell me to just cut her off, but that doesn't feel right to me. I want the connection, but I want the freedom, too."

Step 4: Experience the Feelings of the Unmet Needs

Brian listened to me read back his list of unmet needs, and I asked him how he felt. "Well, I think that I need to . . ." he started.

I tossed him the red-velvet beanbag heart I designed to help people connect with their feelings. "Hang on a minute, Brian. Place this heart on your chest, and close your eyes," I suggested. "Go ahead and sink into your feelings. What is going on for you on the emotional level?"

He took a couple of deep breaths. "This situation feels impossible," he responded.

"So maybe you feel hopeless? Or helpless?" I asked.

"Yes, and most of all, I feel alone and lonely. My sense of integrity wants a different solution than what everyone is recommending to me. Ack! It's too much!"

"Mmm, you sound overwhelmed. And maybe a bit anxious?" I asked.

"Not just a bit anxious, I would say quite stressed, actually," he replied. We both remained quiet for a bit.

Step 5: Connect With the Positive Motivations

"OK, Brian, so at the time you started the relationship with Karen, you had some very good reasons for doing so. Can you recall any of those?" I asked him.

"Yes, absolutely. I believed very strongly that there was something to be gained," he replied.

"And what was that?"

"Learning. Karen is an amazing woman. She is so intelligent but also very spiritual. She is quite successful in work—and she works in a brainy field—but also has a rich inner life. I thought that she was the right woman for me. I knew I wasn't ready, but I was afraid to miss the opportunity—there aren't many single women like her at our age any more. I tried to keep going despite a lack of passion because I thought that passion could grow. Unfortunately, it never did." Brian paused.

"Learning sounds like a very powerful motivator. Any other reasons?" I wondered.

Brian furrowed his eyebrows a bit. "It makes no sense, but I was actually trying to meet my need for integrity. Wait, though—my need for integrity—that need ended up not being met," he said with confusion.

"Right, your need for integrity ended up not being met because of many factors that happened in the situation along the way. But that doesn't mean that it wasn't also one of the original positive motivations. Can you say more about that?" I asked.

"Well, I wanted to commit to what was right. It just felt right to be with a woman who was so together when I was such a mess," he said.

"Committing to what you think is right seems like integrity to me," I finished.

As there were no more additions to this list, I asked Brian to check in with himself in the present moment.

"There is clearly still a lot going on," he said with agitation.

"That's fine," I reassured him. We'll just connect with one pair of feelings and needs at a time."

Step 6: Check In and Make a Request

Brian started with just one feeling:

☑ **OBSERVATIONS:** "In this moment, when I think about having started a relationship with Karen . . ."

☑ **FEELINGS:** "I feel really crappy . . ."

☑ **NEEDS:** "because my need for integrity wasn't met. I just pulled all my old shit," he sighed.

"OK, what else?" I asked.

☑ **FEELINGS:** "Well, I definitely also feel tired and exhausted. I don't want to go through this again. This is the last time!"

☑ **NEEDS:** "I want to capitalize on what I've learned so this doesn't happen ever again, and so I can have more ease, peace, and mental health."

He paused for a moment, looking thoughtful.

☑ **FEELINGS:** "Interesting—now I'm beginning to feel hopeful. I don't need this forever. I can move on from this pattern, and move on from it now."

☑ **NEEDS:** "Wow! I don't mean to sound crass, but that meets a need for efficiency, for Karen as well as myself."

Brian was beginning to look energized.
    "Any other feelings?" I wondered.

☑ **FEELINGS:** "Yes, I feel good, really relaxed. I know that I don't have to respond to that text message."

☑ **NEEDS:** "That meets my needs for rest and ease."

He started to laugh. "It is funny how I worry so much about someone who has a huge capacity to take care of herself."
    "Brian, I wonder if you can think of a request you'd like to make of yourself in regard to this situation?" I prompted.

☑ **REQUESTS:** "Well, I've been going to therapy for about a month now, and my therapist suggests that I give myself a break. When I got Karen's text this morning, I forgot that

I was on break. I want to ask myself to go back on break for as long as I need it. I think this will actually be quite efficient, for me and also for Karen, if I can be clearly on break and not having to respond to her needs. That will stop the cycle of my reaching out to her when I don't really want to," he said with clarity.

I was curious how he felt about responding to Karen's "I miss you" message.

"Actually I don't think it matters." Brian had connected with his feelings and needs, and so was experiencing acceptance of the present moment and the many options available to him. "I'm sure that I can find something appropriate and light to say if I am in the space of giving myself a break. When I do things under pressure, I just screw everything up and the situation gets false or weird. When I return to the feeling of freedom I have when I give myself a break, I just feel like I'm in a flow."

Having heard his request for himself, I asked Brian how he was doing right in the moment.

He beamed. "I feel invigorated and inspired—I wanted to be accountable, and I think that's been taken care of. I've also met my needs for self-connection, self-awareness, and presence."

Graduating From Guilt

Holly Michelle Eckert, CNVC Certified Trainer

Finding Independence

1 What do you feel guilty about?

Having started a romance with Karen.

2 What are you telling yourself you should or shouldn't do?

✓ I shouldn't have started a relationship with her in the beginning.

I shouldn't have led her on.

I should have told her that I didn't need her help.

I shouldn't have accepted her help.

I should have known better.

✓ I should have been more honest with myself.

I should have protected her.

I should have been as attracted to her as she was to me.

3 What needs are not met by the choice you made?

integrity	honesty
community	clarity
ease	support
peace	empathy
fulfillment	

❹ How do you feel when you get in touch with these unmet needs?

hopeless, helpless
alone, lonely
overwhelmed, stressed

❺ What needs were you attempting to meet by the choice you made?

learning
integrity

❻ What are your Observations, Feelings, Needs, and Requests in the present moment?

O   When I think about having started a relationship with Karen,

F   I feel really crappy

N   because my need for integrity wasn't met.

F   I also feel tired and exhausted

N   because I want more ease, peace, and mental health.

F   I'm beginning to feel hopeful

N   about meeting my need for efficiency.

F   I feel good, really relaxed

N   because my needs for rest and ease are met.

R   I want to remind myself to go back "on break," as defined by my therapist, for as long as I need it.

If you still feel guilty, choose another should-statement and repeat steps 3–6.

Liberating Your Power

I met Erika on a trip to Arizona some years ago. Erika was a single mother in her late thirties who had a thirteen-year-old son with both physical and mental disabilities. Her son, Jesse, was in a wheelchair and had the emotional maturity of a four-year-old child. Erika worked during the day while her son was at school and took care of him at nearly all other times. The boy's father had left them, and they had no extended family in town. On the rare occasion that Erika went somewhere other than work, Jesse would scream and cry endlessly at being left with any care provider.

The day I met Erika, however, something else was on her mind. Three days previously, she had put her elderly neighbor's newspaper on the porch railing so the neighbor, Esther, could reach it easily without having to bend down. Erika had then forgotten about Esther until that very morning, when Erika noticed there were two newspapers in the driveway, in addition to the one on the porch railing. Erika called a couple of other neighbors, and the three of them began to talk to Esther through her bedroom window. Esther could not get out of bed but still had enough strength to shout through the closed window. Erika and her neighbors were trying to figure out what to do—wait for a locksmith for up to an hour and a half or call 911 to break down the door. Erika knew that Esther's financial situation could not sustain replacing a door, and Erika's intuition told her that Esther was still OK. After all, if Esther could still shout, she certainly couldn't be near death. Erika called the locksmith to come.

Step 1: Identify the Guilt

"Erika, what specifically do you feel guilty about?" I started.

"I think it comes down to leaving Esther at risk for another hour and a half instead of getting immediate help," she replied.

Step 2: Name the "Shoulds"

"What are you telling yourself that you should or shouldn't have done?"

Erika had a long and immediate list for herself. "Well, first of all, I should have checked on Esther the very first afternoon when the first newspaper wasn't taken in. And then, I definitely should have checked on her the next day, only I just didn't think of it. I should have been thinking of her. I shouldn't have put myself first. I really should be aware of what is going on with others, and I should be a better neighbor."

After Erika paused, I read back the list and asked her which should-statement felt the strongest to her. "I think the thing that gets me the most is that I didn't check on Esther the next day."

Step 3: Connect With the Unmet Needs

I moved Erika into step 3. "So you've got some unmet needs around not having checked on her. Can you connect with what those might be?"

"Sure," she replied. "I need to be a good neighbor."

"Being a good neighbor—do you think that would be a need for community or accountability?" I wondered.

"Both of those," she confirmed. "Needs for attention and awareness, too."

"I'm wondering if you're not experiencing the peace of mind that you'd like as well," I offered.

"Yes, peace," she confirmed. "And maybe more than anything else—integrity—what is the point of acting concerned and then spacing out?"

"Erika, in addition to your own needs, including your need for integrity, would you say that there are some unmet needs in your community, too?" I asked.

Erika looked surprised. "So this can be about unmet needs for others, too? Well, if that's the case, there are many more unmet needs as well, like safety, communication, reliability, and support. Our block had made up an emergency plan that got vetoed by one person who has since moved away, but no one has gotten the ball rolling again."

"What would be the advantages, or met needs, in having that emergency plan?" I prompted.

"It would give us a sense of security and clarity about what to do. For example, if I had a working key to Esther's door, this whole thing wouldn't be a problem. We need to carry through on our responsibility to each other," she said with a great deal of fervor.

Step 4: Experience the Feelings of the Unmet Needs

"Let's sink into the emotions you have in the situation. I'll read your list of unmet needs to you, and just let them enter your heart," I suggested.

When I was done reading the list, I asked Erika how she felt.

She started shaking her hands nervously around her abdominal area. "Uneasy and anxious. Overwhelmed and stressed." She paused for a moment. "Also sad and tired," she added with a sigh.

Step 5: Connect With the Positive Motivations

After a few breaths together in silence, I continued with the process. "Erika, I think you've learned from your reading that one of the fundamental principles in Nonviolent Communication is that every action has a positive motivation. So on that day when you didn't check on Esther, what was motivating you to do the things you chose to do?"

"Selfishness!" she answered, suddenly agitated.

"It doesn't sound like you have a very favorable opinion of that motivation," I said to her, feeling tender. "What if you looked at the situation like this—that there is a positive motivation under any negative motivation? What would be a positive motivation under selfishness? Could you tell me the things you were doing that day?" I asked.

"I was not doing much at all! There I was with my one day off work without my son. I had a million things to do but was doing practically none of them," she answered with both sheepishness and irritation.

"So maybe you were attending to your needs for rest, balance, and self-connection? To have a moment of peace? And perhaps to once again fill your teapot because you know that you're going to be pouring again soon, and you want to make that contribution from a place of love?

"Erika, from what I know about your life with your son, you do an immense amount of contributing with very little community. I can see how you would want to be able to rely on the whole community to support Esther and relieve you of the burden of doing it alone."

"Wow, now that you put it that way, it doesn't seem so selfish," Erika replied, softening. "And on that day off, I wasn't totally lazy. I did make some progress on my papers since my health insurance got wrongly terminated."

"Important needs there!" I affirmed. "A need for order, to get your health insurance back, which will bring you safety, support, and security."

"Hmm . . . maybe a little attention to my own affairs isn't so bad," she concluded with a sweet smile.

Step 6: Check In and Make a Request

"Let's see where you are right now. Can you check in with yourself and determine your Observations, Feelings, Needs, and Requests based on the present moment?" I suggested.

Erika thought for a moment.

☑ **OBSERVATIONS:** "When I recall my decision to wait for the locksmith rather than breaking down Esther's door . . ."

☑ **FEELINGS:** "I feel numbed out . . ."

☑ **NEEDS:** "because I want to protect myself from an overwhelming amount of emotion."

"Yes, that makes sense. Just settle into yourself for another moment. Do you notice any other feelings as well?" I wondered.

☑ **FEELINGS:** "Well, I feel good that I actually took action this morning! My other neighbor saw the newspapers in the driveway but didn't do anything. So I have a tiny amount of appreciation for myself . . ."

☑ **NEEDS:** "because I met my need for competence," she concluded, with a little wink.

"As the last step in the process, can you think of any request you can make of yourself?" I asked.

☑ **REQUESTS:** "Yes. I'd like to get an emergency plan together for our block. We had started before, so the first step would be finding the notes from the previous meetings and asking three people to co-facilitate the committee with me—there is that need for community again! And even just making these plans, I feel empowered."

Graduating From Guilt

Holly Michelle Eckert, CNVC Certified Trainer

Liberating Your Power

1 What do you feel guilty about?

Leaving Esther at risk for the hour and a half it took for the locksmith to come.

2 What are you telling yourself you should or shouldn't do?

I should have checked on her the first afternoon.

✓ I should have checked on her the next day.

I should be thinking about her.

I shouldn't put myself first.

I should be aware of what is going on with others.

I should be a better neighbor.

3 What needs are not met by the choice you made?

community	safety
accountability	communication
attention	reliability
awareness	support
peace of mind	security
integrity	clarity

4   How do you feel when you get in touch with these unmet needs?

uneasy, anxious

overwhelmed, stressed

sad, tired

5   What needs were you attempting to meet by the choice you made?

rest	community
balance	order
self-connection	safety
peace	support
contribution	security
love	

6   What are your Observations, Feelings, Needs, and Requests in the present moment?

O   When I recall my decision to wait for the locksmith,

F   I feel numbed out

N   because I want to protect myself from an overwhelming amount of emotion.

F   I also feel a little appreciation for myself

N   because I met my need for competence.

R   I'm going to get out my notes for the block's emergency plan and ask three people to co-facilitate the committee with me.

If you still feel guilty, choose another should-statement and repeat steps 3–6.

Conclusion

The Gift of Graduating From Guilt

When under a cloud of guilt, we obsess over the details of the past, and thus lose a balanced perspective and limit our access to our innate resourcefulness. In going through the Graduating From Guilt process, the preoccupation with specific past actions falls away, and we instead become inspired to meet needs proactively and comprehensively. The mourning and self-forgiveness steps (steps 3–5) provide the clear and creative state of mind that generates visionary and life-affirming actions. This is the gift of graduating from guilt—finding the action that will restore a sense of empowerment and integrity.

I hope this booklet gives you new ideas and inspires you to benefit from your guilty feelings. When you allow your guilt to guide you to your deepest values, you can take action from a place of self-awareness and be at ease with your integrity. You are then free from blame, and your creativity will flourish.

Graduating From Guilt demonstrates one of the inner uses of NVC. Nonviolent Communication also has numerous applications in the interpersonal realm—in partner relationships, parenting, mediation, social change, and more. For a current listing of book titles, please visit PuddleDancer Press at www.nonviolentcommunication.com.

Graduating From Guilt

Holly Michelle Eckert, CNVC Certified Trainer

1 What do you feel guilty about?

2 What are you telling yourself you should or shouldn't do?

3 What needs are not met by the choice you made?

4 How do you feel when you get in touch with these unmet needs?

5 What needs were you attempting to meet by the choice you made?

6 What are your Observations, Feelings, Needs, and Requests in the present moment?

O

F

N

R

If you still feel guilty, choose another should-statement and repeat steps 3–6.

Index

The Four-Part Nonviolent Communication Process

Clearly expressing how **I am** without blaming or criticizing	Empathically receiving how **you are** without hearing blame or criticism

OBSERVATIONS

1. What I observe *(see, hear, remember, imagine, free from my evaluations)* that does or does not contribute to my well-being:

    "When I (see, hear) . . . "

1. What you observe *(see, hear, remember, imagine, free from your evaluations)* that does or does not contribute to your well-being:

    "When you see/hear . . . "

    (Sometimes unspoken when offering empathy)

FEELINGS

2. How I feel *(emotion or sensation rather than thought)* in relation to what I observe:

    "I feel . . . "

2. How you feel *(emotion or sensation rather than thought)* in relation to what you observe:

    "You feel . . ."

NEEDS

3. What I need or value *(rather than a preference, or a specific action)* that causes my feelings:

    " . . . because I need/value . . . "

3. What you need or value *(rather than a preference, or a specific action)* that causes your feelings:

    " . . . because you need/value . . ."

Clearly requesting that which would enrich **my** life without demanding	Empathically receiving that which would enrich **your** life without hearing any demand

REQUESTS

4. The concrete actions I would like taken:

    "Would you be willing to . . . ?"

4. The concrete actions you would like taken:

    "Would you like . . . ?"

    (Sometimes unspoken when offering empathy)

© Marshall B. Rosenberg. For more information about Marshall B. Rosenberg or the Center for Nonviolent Communication, please visit www.CNVC.org.

Some Basic Feelings We All Have

Feelings when needs are fulfilled

- Amazed
- Comfortable
- Confident
- Eager
- Energetic
- Fulfilled
- Glad
- Hopeful
- Inspired
- Intrigued
- Joyous
- Moved
- Optimistic
- Proud
- Relieved
- Stimulated
- Surprised
- Thankful
- Touched
- Trustful

Feelings when needs are not fulfilled

- Angry
- Annoyed
- Concerned
- Confused
- Disappointed
- Discouraged
- Distressed
- Embarrassed
- Frustrated
- Helpless
- Hopeless
- Impatient
- Irritated
- Lonely
- Nervous
- Overwhelmed
- Puzzled
- Reluctant
- Sad
- Uncomfortable

Some Basic Needs We All Have

Autonomy
- Choosing dreams/goals/values
- Choosing plans for fulfilling one's dreams, goals, values

Celebration
- Celebrating the creation of life and dreams fulfilled
- Celebrating losses: loved ones, dreams, etc. (mourning)

Integrity
- Authenticity • Creativity
- Meaning • Self-worth

Interdependence
- Acceptance • Appreciation
- Closeness • Community
- Consideration
- Contribution to the enrichment of life
- Emotional Safety • Empathy

Physical Nurturance
- Air • Food
- Movement, exercise
- Protection from life-threatening forms of life: viruses, bacteria, insects, predatory animals
- Rest • Sexual Expression
- Shelter • Touch • Water

Play
- Fun • Laughter

Spiritual Communion
- Beauty • Harmony
- Inspiration • Order • Peace

- Honesty (the empowering honesty that enables us to learn from our limitations)
- Love • Reassurance
- Respect • Support
- Trust • Understanding

From the bedroom to the boardroom, from the classroom to the war zone, Nonviolent Communication (NVC) is changing lives every day. NVC provides an easy-to-grasp, effective method to get to the root of violence and pain peacefully. By examining the unmet needs behind what we do and say, NVC helps reduce hostility, heal pain, and strengthen professional and personal relationships. NVC is now being taught in corporations, classrooms, prisons, and mediation centers worldwide. And it is affecting cultural shifts as institutions, corporations, and governments integrate NVC consciousness into their organizational structures and their approach to leadership.

Most of us are hungry for skills that can improve the quality of our relationships, to deepen our sense of personal empowerment or simply help us communicate more effectively. Unfortunately, most of us have been educated from birth to compete, judge, demand, and diagnose; to think and communicate in terms of what is "right" and "wrong" with people. At best, the habitual ways we think and speak hinder communication and create misunderstanding or frustration. And still worse, they can cause anger and pain, and may lead to violence. Without wanting to, even people with the best of intentions generate needless conflict.

NVC helps us reach beneath the surface and discover what is alive and vital within us, and how all of our actions are based on human needs that we are seeking to meet. We learn to develop a vocabulary of feelings and needs that helps us more clearly express what is going on in us at any given moment. When we understand and acknowledge our needs, we develop a shared foundation for much more satisfying relationships. Join the thousands of people worldwide who have improved their relationships and their lives with this simple yet revolutionary process.

About PuddleDancer Press

PuddleDancer Press (PDP) is the premier publisher of Nonviolent Communication™ related works. Its mission is to provide high-quality materials to help people create a world in which all needs are met compassionately. Publishing revenues are used to develop new books, and implement promotion campaigns for NVC and Marshall Rosenberg. By working in partnership with the Center for Nonviolent Communication and NVC trainers, teams, and local supporters, PDP has created a comprehensive promotion effort that has helped bring NVC to thousands of new people each year.

Since 2003 PDP has donated more than 60,000 NVC books to organizations, decision-makers, and individuals in need around the world. This program is supported in part by donations made to CNVC and by partnerships with like-minded organizations around the world. PDP is a core partner of the Help Share NVC Project, giving access to hundreds of valuable tools, resources, and ideas to help NVC trainers and supporters make NVC a household name by creating financially sustainable training practices. Learn more at www.helpsharenvc.com.

Visit the PDP website at www.NonviolentCommunication.com to find the following resources:

- **Shop NVC**—Continue your learning. Purchase our NVC titles online safely, affordably, and conveniently. Find everyday discounts on individual titles, multiple-copies, and book packages. Learn more about our authors and read endorsements of NVC from world-renowned communication experts and peacemakers.

- **NVC Quick Connect e-Newsletter**—Sign up today to receive our monthly e-Newsletter, filled with expert articles, upcoming training opportunities with our authors, and exclusive specials on NVC learning materials. Archived e-Newsletters are also available

- **About NVC**—Learn more about these life-changing communication and conflict resolution skills including an overview of the NVC process, key facts about NVC, and more.

- **About Marshall Rosenberg**—Access press materials, biography, and more about this world-renowned peacemaker, educator, bestselling author, and founder of the Center for Nonviolent Communication.

- **Free Resources for Learning NVC**—Find free weekly tips series, NVC article archive, and other great resources to make learning these vital communication skills just a little easier.

 PuddleDancer P R E S S

For more information, please contact PuddleDancer Press at:

P.O. Box 231129 • Encinitas CA 92024
Phone: 858-759-6963 • Fax: 858-759-6967
Email: email@puddledancer.com • www.NonviolentCommunication.com

About the Center for Nonviolent Communication

The Center for Nonviolent Communication (CNVC) is an international nonprofit peacemaking organization whose vision is a world where everyone's needs are met peacefully. CNVC is devoted to supporting the spread of Nonviolent Communication (NVC) around the world.

Founded in 1984 by Dr. Marshall B. Rosenberg, CNVC has been contributing to a vast social transformation in thinking, speaking and acting— showing people how to connect in ways that inspire compassionate results. NVC is now being taught around the globe in communities, schools, prisons, mediation centers, churches, businesses, professional conferences, and more. More than 200 certified trainers and hundreds more teach NVC to approximately 250,000 people each year in 35 countries.

CNVC believes that NVC training is a crucial step to continue building a compassionate, peaceful society. Your tax-deductible donation will help CNVC continue to provide training in some of the most impoverished, violent corners of the world. It will also support the development and continuation of organized projects aimed at bringing NVC training to high-need geographic regions and populations.

To make a tax-deductible donation or to learn more about the valuable resources described below, visit the CNVC website at www.CNVC.org:

- **Training and Certification**—Find local, national, and international training opportunities, access trainer certification information, connect to local NVC communities, trainers, and more.

- **CNVC Bookstore**—Find mail or phone order information for a complete selection of NVC books, booklets, audio, and video materials at the CNVC website.

- **CNVC Projects**—Seven regional and theme-based projects provide focus and leadership for teaching NVC in a particular application or geographic region.

- **E-Groups and List Servs**—Join one of several moderated, topic-based NVC e-groups and list servs developed to support individual learning and the continued growth of NVC worldwide.

For more information, please contact CNVC at:

 5600 San Francisco Rd. NE Suite A, Albuquerque, NM 87109
Ph: 505-244-4041 • Fax: 505-247-0414
Email: cnvc@CNVC.org • Website: www.CNVC.org

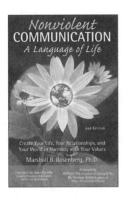

Nonviolent Communication:
A Language of Life, Second Edition

*Create Your Life, Your Relationships, and Your World
in Harmony with Your Values*

Marshall B. Rosenberg, Ph.D.

$19.95 — Trade Paper 6x9, 240pp

ISBN: 978-1-892005-03-8

In this internationally acclaimed text, Marshall Rosenberg offers insightful stories, anecdotes, practical exercises and role-plays that will literally change your approach to communication for the better. Nonviolent Communication partners practical skills with a powerful consciousness to help us get what we want peacefully.

Discover how the language you use can strengthen your relationships, build trust, prevent or resolve conflicts peacefully, and heal pain. More than 400,000 copies of this landmark text have been sold in twenty languages around the globe.

"Nonviolent Communication is a simple yet powerful methodology for communicating in a way that meets both parties' needs. This is one of the most useful books you will ever read."

—William Ury, coauthor of *Getting to Yes* and author of *The Third Side*

"I believe the principles and techniques in this book can literally change the world, but more importantly, they can change the quality of your life with your spouse, your children, your neighbors, your co-workers, and everyone else you interact with."

—Jack Canfield, author, *Chicken Soup for the Soul*

Nonviolent Communication
Companion Workbook

*A Practical Guide for Individual,
Group, or Classroom Study*

by Lucy Leu

$21.95 — Trade Paper 7x10, 224pp

ISBN: 978-1-892005-04-5

Learning Nonviolent Communication has often been equated with learning a whole new language. The *NVC Companion Workbook* helps you put these powerful, effective skills into practice with chapter-by-chapter study of Marshall Rosenberg's cornerstone text, *NVC: A Language of Life*. Create a safe, supportive group learning or practice environment that nurtures the needs of each participant. Find a wealth of activities, exercises, and facilitator suggestions to refine and practice this powerful communication process.

**Available from PDP, CNVC, all major bookstores, and Amazon.com
Distributed by IPG: 800-888-4741**

Being Me, Loving You • *A Practical Guide to Extraordinary Relationships* **by Marshall B. Rosenberg, Ph.D.** • Watch your relationships strengthen as you learn to think of love as something you "do," something you give freely from the heart. 80pp, ISBN: 978-1-892005-16-8 • **$8.95**

Getting Past the Pain Between Us • *Healing and Reconciliation Without Compromise* **by Marshall B. Rosenberg, Ph.D.** • Learn simple steps to create the heartfelt presence necessary for lasting healing to occur—great for mediators, counselors, families, and couples. 48pp, ISBN: 978-1-892005-07-6 • **$8.95**

The Heart of Social Change • *How to Make a Difference in Your World* **by Marshall B. Rosenberg, Ph.D.** • Learn how creating an internal consciousness of compassion can impact your social change efforts. 48pp, ISBN: 978-1-892005-10-6 • **$8.95**

Parenting From Your Heart • *Sharing the Gifts of Compassion, Connection, and Choice* **by Inbal Kashtan** • Filled with insight and practical skills, this booklet will help you transform your parenting to address every day challenges. 48pp, ISBN: 978-1-892005-08-3 • **$8.95**

Practical Spirituality • *Reflections on the Spiritual Basis of Nonviolent Communication* **by Marshall B. Rosenberg, Ph.D.** • Marshall's views on the spiritual origins and underpinnings of NVC, and how practicing the process helps him connect to the Divine. 48pp, ISBN: 978-1-892005-14-4 • **$8.95**

Raising Children Compassionately • *Parenting the Nonviolent Communication Way* **by Marshall B. Rosenberg, Ph.D.** • Learn to create a mutually respectful, enriching family dynamic filled with heartfelt communication. 32pp, ISBN: 978-1-892005-09-0 • **$7.95**

The Surprising Purpose of Anger • *Beyond Anger Management: Finding the Gift* **by Marshall B. Rosenberg, Ph.D.** • Marshall shows you how to use anger to discover what you need, and then how to meet your needs in more constructive, healthy ways. 48pp, ISBN: 978-1-892005-15-1 • **$8.95**

Teaching Children Compassionately • *How Students and Teachers Can Succeed with Mutual Understanding* **by Marshall B. Rosenberg, Ph.D.** • In this national keynote address to Montessori educators, Marshall describes his progressive, radical approach to teaching that centers on compassionate connection. 48pp, ISBN: 978-1-892005-11-3 • **$8.95**

We Can Work It Out • *Resolving Conflicts Peacefully and Powerfully* **by Marshall B. Rosenberg, Ph.D.** • Practical suggestions for fostering empathic connection, genuine co-operation, and satisfying resolutions in even the most difficult situations. 32pp, ISBN: 978-1-892005-12-0 • **$7.95**

What's Making You Angry? • *10 Steps to Transforming Anger So Everyone Wins* **by Shari Klein and Neill Gibson** • A powerful, step-by-step approach to transform anger to find healthy, mutually satisfying outcomes. 32pp, ISBN: 978-1-892005-13-7 • **$7.95**

Available from PDP, CNVC, all major bookstores, and Amazon.com. Distributed by IPG: 800-888-4741. For more information about these booklets or to order online, visit www.NonviolentCommunication.com

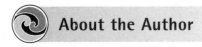

About the Author

Holly Michelle Eckert, in 1999, first felt the power of Nonviolent Communication (NVC) as a way to increase the effectiveness and enjoyment of her parenting. Within an hour of beginning to read Marshall Rosenberg's *Nonviolent Communication: A Language of Life,* she was clear that sharing NVC would be her primary gift to the world.

By 2001, Holly was teaching these skills to other parents as Director of Northwest Attachment Parenting. However, her passion for NVC extended far beyond its usefulness in parenting. She knew that NVC transforms all types of relationships, and over the next few years, crafted a sequence of Nonviolent Communication courses into her *Radiant Relationships Seminar Series,* now available both as live seminars and online self-study classes.

Holly has a keen interest in the spiritual realm, having studied energy medicine and shamanism. Various teachings from these fields wind their way into the courses as well.

Formerly a teacher of music pedagogy and faculty member at Alfred University and Hamilton College, Holly displays a deep understanding of the artistry of teaching. Her teaching is described as perfectly balanced between structured and spontaneous, deep yet light-hearted. Her focus is to make NVC universally accessible, fool-proof, and uplifting.

Holly loves to create beauty in many forms. Over the course of a day, she may experience an exquisite moment of intimacy with one of her children, cook a gourmet meal, and knit a few rows on a mohair shawl. Holding a Doctorate in Music from the Eastman School of Music, Holly also delights audiences with jazz and classical performances on both violin and piano.